THE LEGAL ETHIC
FRANKLY, MR. SIMONE, YOU'RE GUILTY OF ONE OF THE MOST HEINOUS, INHUMAN, DESPICABLE CRIMES EVER COMMITTED! NOTHING COULD CONVINCE ME TO DEFEND YOU!
I'LL PAY IN CASH.
I'LL TAKE YOUR CASE.

THE ROMANTIC LAWYER
LISTEN! ON THE ROOF! IT'S RAINING. HOW ROMANTIC!
YEAH.
...EXTRA...
RAIN RESPONSIBLE FOR 138 CAR ACCIDENTS
EXTRA
RAIN BLAMED
RECORD CAR ACCIDENTS

A LAWYER LULLING HIMSELF TO SLEEP
ALIMONY SETTLEMENT
PERSONAL INJURY SETTLEMENT
GROSS NEGLIGENCE SETTLEMENT

THE COMPASSIONATE SOLICITOR
GO AHEAD AND CRY, MRS. DUNNE. HERE, HAVE A TISSUE... ONLY 35 PENCE
SOB SOB
LAW

THE LAST REQUEST
YOU ROTTEN SHYSTER! YOU'VE DRAGGED THIS OUT OVER FOURTEEN YEARS OF APPEALS AND THROUGH HUNDREDS OF THOUSANDS OF MY POUNDS; AND HERE I SIT, RIGHT WHERE I STARTED. WHAT MORE COULD YOU POSSIBLY WANT OUTTA ME?!
HOW ABOUT THE RIGHTS TO YOUR LIFE STORY? BE A SWEETHEART, SIGN HERE.

THE DIVORCE SETTLEMENT
"HIS" SHARE
"HER" SHARE
THE LAWYERS' SHARE

THE "LEGAL AID" LAWYER
THE WAY I SEE IT, MR. GOMEZ, YOU'D BEST PLEAD GUILTY TO THE MANSLAUGHTER CHARGES WHICH COULD NET YOU SIX TO TEN YEARS, TOPS.
WHAT MANSLAUGHTER?! I'M HERE TO SUE MY LANDLORD!!

THE SPECIALIST SERVICE
"Our Lawyers can relate to your particular problem."
MOST OF THEM HAVE BEEN IN JAIL, TOO.

THE CHRISTENING OF A FUTURE LAWYER
HEY! WATCH THE ROBE, YOU! YOU STAIN THIS SUIT AND I'LL HAUL YOU INTO COURT QUICKER'N YOU CAN SAY "AMEN, BROTHER".

GETTING A MALPRACTICE SUIT TO TRIAL: STEP 1
WE'LL SUE THE DOCTOR FOR THE FATAL BLUNDER IN YOUR OPERATION MR. SNORDFICK, FOR £2-3 MILLION!
BUT I HAVE NO FAMILY AND I WON'T LIVE TO SPEND THE MONEY!
ALWAYS THINKING OF YOURSELF! WHAT ABOUT MY FAMILY?! MY CHILDREN HAVE TO EAT, YOU KNOW!
YOU'RE RIGHT, MR. PALMDWARF, HOW THOUGHTLESS OF ME.

IF LAWYERS WROTE THE TRAFFIC SIGNS:
THE PARTY OF THE FIRST PART SHALL YIELD TO THE PARTY OF THE SECOND PART.
CEASE AND DESIST
NO RIGHT TURN PER SE

NEW LAWYER AD · I
"I got rid of 187lbs. of ugly fat."
"With the help of Snooks, Freize, & Mulch, Solicitors I divorced him."
BEFORE
AFTER

PROBATE.
WELL, MR. NOONTZ, AFTER PROBATE, COURT COSTS, TAXES, ETC., YOUR £50,000 INHERITANCE WORKS OUT TO BE £937.
£937!!
AND HERE'S MY BILL FOR £1200

AN EFFECTIVE "OPENING STATEMENT"
HEY, BABE. I'D LIKE TO DO TO YOU WHAT THE LEGAL PROFESSION HAS DONE TO THIS COUNTRY.
OH, WOW.

YOUR ONE PHONE CALL
HELLO. THIS IS MARSHALL SMURTZ, SOLICITOR. I'M NOT IN RIGHT NOW. I'M ON A THREE WEEK CARIBBEAN CRUISE ABOARD MY NEW YACHT. HOWEVER, IF YOU LEAVE A MESSAGE AT THE BEEP...

THE OUT-OF-COURT SETTLEMENT
OUR COMPANY IS PREPARED TO OFFER YOUR CLIENT £150,000 AS AN OUT-OF-COURT SETTLEMENT ON THIS CASE.
£150,000? A RATHER PALTRY SUM. HOWEVER, WE WOULD LIKE TO DICUSS YOUR OFFER IN PRIVATE, IF YOU DON'T MIND...
WOW WEE 150 G'S !!
HOT-CHA-CHA! WOOO-WHEEE!

THE BENEVOLENT LAWYER
FOR THIS TYPE OF CASE, MISS DYNELLE, I NORMALLY CHARGE HEH, HEH... £1500. BUT BECAUSE YOU HAVE SUCH A WARM, SINCERE, FRIENDLY LITTLE, ER, SMILE, MY FEE WILL BE £250.

THE HOLIDAY SPIRIT
THAT'S RIGHT, MR. SPIVEY. I'M JUST CALLING TO WISH YOU A WARM AND CHEERFUL HOLIDAY!
MISS HARKEY, CHARGE THIS CALL TO THE SPIVEY ACCOUNT.

"ENTERTAINMENT BUSINESS" LAWYERS
HEY, SID, YOU'RE BEAUTIFUL.
BARRY, YOU'RE BEAUTIFUL, REALLY.
SOL, YOU'RE A BEAUTIFUL GUY.
HEY, MARTY, YOU'RE BEAUTIFUL.
YOU'RE BEAUTIFUL, JERRY.
GENE, YOU'RE BEAUTIFUL, REALLY.
WE'LL DO LUNCH SOON. OKAY, ABE?
AL, YOU'RE BEAUTIFUL!

FIRST YEAR LAW SCHOOL STUDENTS

NEW SOLICITORS' AD • II
BE AN INSTANT MULTI-MILLIONAIRE!
LIKE MR. AND MRS. DARVEL CARNEY OF WEST WYCOMBE
"YES, IT'S TRUE! WITH THE EXPERT HELP OF OUR LAWYERS LANGTON, FITCH, AND BOSCO, WE SUED OUR DOCTORS FOR MALPRACTICE AND COLLECTED OVER TWO MILLION POUNDS!"
AND YOU CAN, TOO; WITH OUR HELP.
Langton, Fitch, & Bosco
"BECAUSE WE KNOW WHAT IT TAKES TO TAKE SOMEONE TO THE CLEANERS."

THE ADVOCATE OF JUSTICE
GOOD NEWS, CHIGGERS! BECAUSE YOU'VE TURNED QUEEN'S EVIDENCE, THE JUDGE HAS KNOCKED YOUR TRIPLE MURDER CHARGE DOWN TO A £100 FINE.
UNT. UNT, UNT.
B76294

TWO LAW OFFICES
LAW CENTRE
PARKING FOR EMPLOYEES ONLY
LAVIN, GLATT, DITMAN, & STABB
701
LAW OFFICE
PERSONAL INJURY
A SPECIALITY
GLATT
DITMAN

THE "NO RISK" CASE: IMMIGRATION
YOU DISHONOURABLE LAWYERS! YOU ARE TAKING OUR MONEY AND WHAT ARE WE GETTING?
DEPORTED!
BYE-BYE.
TRAPDOOR
TRAPDOOR RELEASE

ANNUAL CONVENTION OF BARRISTERS

LAWYERS' TRACK-AND-FIELD EVENT
SLIP AND FALL HEATS
SQUIRT
ACH! MY BACK!
UHH! OOOOOF!

THE NOTORIOUS CASE
MR. CRUSHNIC, YOU'RE REPRESENTING MR. PITZLE, A KNOWN CRIMINAL, WHO IS SUING HIS MUGGING VICTIM BECAUSE, WHILE IN THE COURSE OF THE CRIME, THE VICTIM BROKE PITZLE'S ARM AND NOW PITZLE CLAIMS HE'S BEEN DENIED HIS ONLY SOURCE OF LIVELIHOOD AND WANTS ONE MILLION POUNDS IN DAMAGES. WHY WOULD AN ATTORNEY OF YOUR STATURE HANDLE SUCH A CASE?
PUBLICITY.

THE SUCCESSFUL BARRISTER

THE VERY SUCCESSFUL BARRISTER
AMBULANCE
AMBULANCE
AMBULANCE
AMBULANCE

A FUTURE LAWYER AT PLAY
ERRRRRRRR...
PUZZLE
AMBULANCE
AMBULANCE
AMBULANCE
AMBULANCE
AMBULANCE
AMBULANCE

THREE MOTHERS
MY SON THE SURGEON HAS DEVELOPED A NEW ARTIFICIAL HEART VALVE THAT WILL SAVE THE LIVES OF COUNTLESS CARDIAC PATIENTS!
MY SON THE SCIENTIST HAS DEVELOPED A NEW FOODSTUFF CAPABLE OF FEEDING THOUSANDS OF PEOPLE FOR UNDER FIVE POUNDS!
MY SON THE LAWYER HAS DEVELOPED A UNIQUE BILLING SYSTEM WHICH ALLOWS HIM TO BILL CLIENTS FOR TIME HE SPENDS ON THE GOLF COURSE!

THE BAR EXAM
TAKING THE BAR, HUH? RIGHT AFTER I TOOK IT IN '54, I HAD TO BE HOSPITALIZED FOR NERVOUS EXHAUSTION.
MY LAW PARTNER'S SON FAILED IT SIXTEEN TIMES, THEN COMMITTED SUICIDE.
NO SMOKING IN ELEVATOR
I SEE YOU'RE TAKING YOUR OWN ELECTRIC TYPEWRITER. I HOPE THERE'S NOT A POWER FAILURE LIKE LAST YEAR.
MY EX-ROOMMATE'S BEEN TAKING IT SINCE 1962.
YEAH, AND IT GETS TOUGHER AND TOUGHER EVERY YEAR!

AN IMPORTANT PHONE INTERRUPTION
THEN, AFTER HE SLAPPED ME AROUND FOR AWHILE, HE KIDNAPPED OUR LITTLE DAUGHTER AND...
EXCUSE ME, MRS. BENSON. I MUST TAKE THIS IMPORTANT CALL...
...HELLO, GUIDO? I'VE DECIDED ON THE ROYAL BLUE TERRA-COTTA TILES FOR MY NEW BATHROOM

A LAWYER AT THE MOVIES
AS OF THIS MINUTE, RONALD, OUR AFFAIR IS HISTORY.
WHAT DOES SHE MEAN BY THAT, CLAYTON?
SHE MEANS THAT SHE ELECTS TO TERMINATE THEIR RELATIONSHIP ENTIRELY, OR SO MUCH OF IT AS REMAINS UNPERFORMED, DOING AWAY WITH EXISTING AGREEMENT UNDER AGREED TERMS AND CONSEQUENCES.

CREATIVE BILLING #7

A MONUMENT TO ALL THE HONEST LAWYERS-TURNED-POLITICIANS
TO BE ERECTED WHEN WE FIND ONE.

A LAWYER TO THE RESCUE
HELP ME!! HELP ME!!
YEAH, SURE. HERE'S MY CARD.
CALUCCI'S GROCERIES

UNFORESEEN ADDITIONAL COSTS
YOUR BILL IS £75 MORE THAN WE ESTIMATED, MRS. MUNSKI, DUE TO UNFORESEEN INVESTIGATIVE RESEARCH, ADDITIONAL FILING FEES, COURT COSTS, ETC.
SPORTING GOODS
SALE
PRO MODEL
£75

TRYING TO SUE YOUR SOLICITOR
I'D LIKE TO SEE A LAWYER ABOUT BRINGING SUIT AGAINST MY OWN LAWYER.

THE LAWYER AT THE FIRST THANKSGIVING
YAACH! GAG! GAG! THERE'S A TURKEY BONE IN THE STUFFING! WHO'S RESPONSIBLE?! I HOPE YOU'RE INSURED FOR THIS! I'LL -GAG- SUE! - GAG!

SPOTTING THE LAWYERS IN A CROWDED RESTAURANT

THE BAR COUNCIL REPRIMANDING ONE OF ITS MEMBERS'

THE BAR COUNCIL SEVERELY REPRIMANDING ONE OF ITS MEMBERS
Z

AN ATTORNEY AT AN ORGY
WHIPLASH!!

STUPID QUESTION #55
DON'T WORRY, RONNY. WE'LL HAVE YOU OUT OF HERE FIRST THING IN THE MORNING. ARE YOU GOING TO BE OKAY??

NEW LAWYERS AD • III
INOPERABLE? TERMINAL? FATAL?
ABOUT TO KICK THE BUCKET?
DON'T GO UNPREPARED;
WITH YOUR LEGAL AFFAIRS
STILL A MESS!
CALL THE LEGAL OFFICES OF
DUNKLE, PIGEON, & VEEZY
HOSPITAL

THE HOURLY RATE
WELL, MR. CAPUTO, MY HOURLY RATE IS £35...
SCUSI, MA NON PARLO INGLESE MOLTO BENE, SIGNORE.
I SEE. AS I WAS SAYING, MY HOURLY RATE IS £55...

EVERY LAWYER'S GOAL
LIZ! LIZ! COME QUICKLY! I FINALLY DID IT! I HAVE ALL SIXTEEN PHONE LINES ON HOLD! SIXTEEN IMPORTANT CLIENTS, ALL ON HOLD!! HOT DAMN!!
OH... UH...GREAT.

THE LAWYER'S SPOUSE
HONEY, HAVE YOU COLLECTED THE SETTLEMENT ON THAT CLIENT OF YOURS WHO LOST HIS ARM?
NOT YET, DEAR. WHY?
BECAUSE, WELL, WE COULD USE A NEW BEDROOM SUITE.
SPORTS

A LAWYER'S FREUDIAN SLIP
YES, OF COURSE YOU HAVE A VALID CASE, MRS. PEENABORDLE; AND WE'LL SUE THE S.O.B.s TO GET WHAT'S RIGHTFULLY MINE... ER... YOURS.

THE SENIOR PARTNER'S OFFICE
OUR FIRST PILE

CONVINCING AN "EXPERT WITNESS" TO TESTIFY

THE EXPERT WITNESS'S TESTIMONY
...AND SO THE INFRACTION OF PALLIATIVE TREATMENT PREEMPTS THE PHYSIOLOGICAL SUBDIVISIONS OF ACUTE MYASTHENIA CAUSED BY AN EXCESS OF LINE GREMLINS.
THEREFORE, DOCTOR, WHEN THE DEFENDANT STABBED HIS VICTIM TWENTY-TWO TIMES IN THE BACK, IN YOUR PROFESSIONAL OPINION, IT WAS INDEED AN ACCIDENT.
ABSOLUTELY.

CREATIVE BILLING #16
MILLIE, CHARGE THREE HOURS OF MY TIME TO MRS. BELASCO'S ACCOUNT. WE DISCUSSED HER CASE AT LUNCH TODAY.
...SPEAKING OF BIG HOOTERS! YOU SHOULD SEE THE ONES ON THIS BELASCO BROAD!!!!

PROTECTING ONE'S HOME FROM LAWYERS
NOT RESPONSIBLE FOR FALLING BRANCHES OR BIRD DOO.
NOT RESPONSIBLE FOR FALLING SLATES
NOT RESPONSIBLE FOR GUTTER FALLING ON HEAD
WATCH OUT FOR CRACK! NOT RESPONSIBLE FOR TRIPS!
WARNING: ENTER AT OWN RISK!
BEWARE OF DOG. OWNER NOT RESPONSIBLE FOR MAULING
WARNING: NOT RESPONSIBLE FOR ANYTHING
NO TRESPASSING
WALK UP PATH AT OWN RISK.
SLIPPERY WHEN WET; GRITTY WHEN DRY
NOT RESPONSIBLE FOR GRASS STAINS INCURRED

NEW LAWYER'S AD · IV
DEAD MAN'S CURVE
CONGRATULATIONS! IF YOU'RE READING THIS, YOU'VE SURVIVED!
AND YOU REALLY NEED LEGAL AID:
"BUTCHIE FENSTER LAW SERVICE"
PERSONAL INJURY · GROSS NEGLIGENCE
OUR MOTTO IS
"WE'LL GET 'EM ON FACTORY DEFECTS."

PUTTING IT SIMPLY
SO, CONTRACTS OF RECORD ARE SUCH AS DECLARED AND ADJUDICATED BY COURTS OF COMPETENT JURISDICTION, OR ENTERED ON THEIR RECORDS, INCLUDING JUDGEMENTS, RECOGNIZANCES, AND FORCE STATUTES...
IN CASE OF EMERGENCY, BREAK GLASS
DICTIONARY

THE LAWYER IN CHILDREN'S LITERATURE
HI, KIDS! TIRED? LOST? CUSTODY PROBLEMS? COME INSIDE. WE'LL TALK.
LEVERDA SHULTZ LAWYER
SPECIALIZING IN FAMILY LAW + DIVORCE

A LAWYER AT THE BEACH
MY CARD.

A LAWYER'S SOUND ADVICE
OH MY GOD! HAROLD! THAT TIE! I TOLD YOU NOT TO WEAR A LOUD TIE. HOW DO YOU EXPECT ME TO CONVINCE A JURY OF YOUR INNOCENCE WHEN YOU WEAR A TIE LIKE THAT? I MIGHT AS WELL WASH MY HANDS OF THIS WHOLE CASE RIGHT NOW! DON'T BLAME ME IF THEY GIVE YOU LIFE FOR THIS!

LAWYERS AT A CHAPEL OF REST
ARE YOU GUYS GOING TO MAKE ANYTHING OFF THIS?
YEAH. I'M HANDLING THE ESTATE.
I'M HANDLING THE INSURANCE CLAIM.
I THOUGHT I'D CHECK HIS SUIT POCKETS FOR ANY LOOSE CHANGE.

A DOCTOR'S NIGHTMARE (A LAWYER'S DREAM)
AHA! X-RAYS SHOW THAT YOU LEFT A CLAMP INSIDE MRS. FERNNIE AFTER SURGERY!!!!
MALPRACTICE! MALPRACTICE! 8...9...10 MILLION.!!!
OH NO! NO! NO! NO! NO! NO! NO! NO...

THE JUNIOR PARTNER
"I CAME. I SAW. I CONCURRED."

A NICE GESTURE
YOUR CLIENT, MR. GROVER, LEFT HIS RAINCOAT HERE.
AS A NICE GESTURE, MISS SLATZ, SEND IT OUT TO BE CLEANED; THEN HAVE IT SENT TO GROVER'S HOUSE.
BE SURE TO MARK UP THE CLEANING AND DELIVERY FEES 100% AND CHARGE IT TO HIS ACCOUNT.

ALWAYS PREPARED
YOU DIDN'T TELL ME SHE WAS PREGNANT.
YES I DID.
YOU DIDN'T MENTION THE QUICK DIVORCE.
YES I DID.
THERE'S QUITE A BIT YOU HAVEN'T TOLD ME, MR. TYLER.
MY NAME IS STEINER!

IF LAWYERS WROTE FOR THE MOVIES
BUT, RHETT! IF YOU GO, WHERE SHALL I GO? WHAT SHALL I DO?
FRANKLY, MY DEAR, RES IPSA LOQUITUR.

A LAWYER AT A PARTY
SAY, DOC, I'VE BEEN FEELING KIND OF DIZZY IN THE MORNING. WHAT COULD BE CAUSING IT?
DEPENDS, BERNIE. ARE YOU HAVING ANY TROUBLE SLEEPING, OR ARE...
SAY, FLO, I'VE BEEN THINKING ABOUT INVESTING IN COMMODITIES. HOW DOES GOLD LOOK?
IT'LL PROBABLY CONTINUE TO DROP UNTIL APRIL, THEN MAKE A STRONG COMEBACK...
SAY, TIM, THIS GUY WANTS TO SELL ME HIS '67 JAGUAR FOR £2,000. IS THAT A GOOD PRICE?
WELL, BERNIE, GLASS'S GUIDE ON A '67 IN MINT CONDITION IS ABOUT...
HEY, BERNIE MY NEIGHBOUR IS THREATENING TO SUE ME IF I DON'T...
HEY! WHADDAYA THINK THIS IS, FREE LEGAL AID!?! IF YOU WANT LEGAL ADVICE, CALL MY SECRETARY FOR AN APPOINTMENT!!!

TWO ATTORNEYS MAKING LOVE
HOW WOULD YOU LIKE A LITTLE TICKLE RIGHT THERE?!
OBJECTION!
SUSTAINED. YOU DO LIKE THIS SPOT, THOUGH, DON'T YOU?
OBJECTION. CALLS FOR A CONCLUSION.
OVERRULED!

GOVERNMENT LAWYERS

A LAWYER READING TO HIS CHILDREN
AND THEN JACK—WHO AT THIS TIME WAS ALREADY GUILTY OF TRESPASSING AND BREAKING AND ENTERING—SNATCHED THE GOOSE THAT LAID THE GOLDEN EGGS—THUS ADDING BURGLARY TO HIS GROWING LIST OF MALICIOUS FELONIES.
Z
JACK AND THE BEANSTALK

AT HOME WITH THE LAST HONEST, ETHICAL LAWYERS

THE FUTURE LAWYER AT PLAY
DUCK...
DUCK...
DUCK...
DUCK...
GOOSE!
WHACK!
AAACHH! MY NECK! MY FACE! IT'S PARALYZED! I'LL SUE!!!

A LAWYERS' RUNNING RACE
AMBULANCE

AN OBSCENE PHONE CALL FROM A LAWYER
MMM... UH!... I WANT TO PERFORM... ...PANT, PANT... SERIOUS AND WILFUL MISCONDUCT ON YOUR... PANT... CORPUS DELICTI DURING... MMM... AN INDICTABLE OFFENCE

THE TAX SPECIALIST
RIBS
STENTZMAN & THORK
TAX REPRESENTATION
FULL SERVICE
•TAX RETURN PREPARATION
•BUSINESS TRANSACTIONS
•ONE-WAY TICKETS TO BRAZIL

GUESS WHICH OF THESE PEOPLE HAVE CONSULTED LAWYERS?
TRAFFIC COURT

WHEN LAWYERS ADVERTISE ON TV
HEY!! FOR A REAL DEAL, COME ON DOWN TO AL BENDERS LAW FIRM! HAVE A LOOK AT THIS LADY'S DIVORCE COST HER ONLY £179.99 AT AL'S!
THIS HERE EX-CON'S DEFENCE ON A BURGLARY CHARGE SET HIM BACK ONLY £49.99!
DEALS GALORE AT AL'S !!!
COMPLETE DIVORCE! £179.99
BURGLARY CHARGE £49.99
AL BENDER'S CUT-RATE LEGAL FEES
PROBATE! £89.99
MOTORWAY AHEAD

RECOGNIZING THE CRIMINAL
CON-ARTIST
LAWYER

2.50

NO GOOD LAWYERS

by Rick Detorie

ORBIS · LONDON

First published in the United States by Pocket Books, a division of Simon & Schuster Inc, New York
This edition published in the United Kingdom by Orbis Publishing Limited, London 1985

Printed in Great Britain
ISBN 0 85613 813 4